HUNDERTWASSER

WERNER HOFMANN

HUNDERTWASSER

VERLAG GALERIE WELZ SALZBURG

Translated from the German by Della Couling.
Distributed in England by Graffiti Fair, London.

A spiral runs in two directions: either away from the centre or towards it, and the eye of the observer can follow the same course. But whether it decides in favour of dilation or contraction, expansion or concentration, is left to us: the eye can just as easily wander into the linear framework as out of it.

Hundertwasser has become known as the painter of spirals, a fame he has justly earned with this identification mark, for he has proved capable of mastering the ambivalence of that ancient motif. Such a statement expresses a psychologising supposition and suggests that the choice of motif is not meant-merely to illustrate his inclination for a particular form; nor has it originated merely from the artist's admiration for the Viennese art nouveau movement, the art of the "Secession". It is true that Hundertwasser has often stated that he feels indebted to the highly intricate style of Klimt and Schiele (and by so saying, incidentally, he has made an international public familiar with names which that public — until very recently — was scarcely aware of), nevertheless his spiral-mania should be understood not merely as artistic homage to two "masters", but as revealing a central human disposition: a disposition which lives on contrasts, in other words plans tensions within itself.

Thus we find a need to expand, an urge to spread out, in order to obtain in the truest sense of the word a "comprehensive" space for visualizing; a desire to impress on the world an action trail. A communicative urge of this kind can assume the most varied forms and often lapse into exhibitionism. One man may tattoo his ideals on his body, another may promulgate himself by putting his name on every available object (Kieselack). Hundertwasser's experiment of painting one room of the Hamburg Art Academy with a spiral is another example, as also the painted chair (in a Viennese private collection), or the "Verschimmelungsmanifest", in which he wrote: "A man in an apartment house must have the possibility of leaning out of his window and — as far as his hands can reach — scratching off the masonry. And he must be allowed to take a long brush and paint everything pink — as far as he can reach — so that from far off, from the street, everyone can see that in that apartment lives a man who is different from his neighbours, the tame cattle." The creative act as self-affirmation and as self-activation: the world belongs to me, as far as my arm can reach. Hundertwasser would like to show the cattle the way out of the paddock. He proclaims, in theory at least, that everything that comes within the range of his brush must reckon on being changed in colour. The formal analogy of this expansive urge to communicate is the spiral. In it lies too the motif of perpetual, uninterrupted activity, of manic restlessness: the opening spiral never comes to an end. Its course is occupied in a curious way with itself: by opening itself and gaining new territory, it nevertheless still ceaselessly circles round itself, watches its own past, can never break free from the soliloquy and indeed may not, for by so doing it would lose what constitutes its individuality. Every new rotation twines in characteristic self-love round its predecessor. Thus the spiral becomes a visual metaphor of Narcissus.

Interpreted in the opposite sense, the spiral signifies a gradual narrowing, a contraction, a retreat into a nuclear zone, which is slowly encircled and cocooned. In such a way the lines with which Hundertwasser duly transformed an academy room into a casing can be explained in their protective function, as a shielding from the outside world: they form a spun cocoon and at the same time turn the smooth-walled box-room into a cave-like dwelling, an architectural body, offering a haven.

That is the other, fragile side of Narcissus: his flight from the world, a flight which has its origin in fear of the world, in an extreme vulnerability and susceptibility of his psychic make-up. And yet this cocooning of oneself cannot do without expansion, just as nuclear zone and periphery, inside and outside, are mutually dependent. Only the expansively outward wandering line movement succeeds therefore in transforming outer world into inner world.

The double motif of circling both outwards and inwards offers the key to the double meaning of this image world. A spontaneous mobility which appears to be inexhaustible is peculiar to lines. It runs in fine rills which seem to have no end. At the same time however these line-threads constantly try to incapsulate one another, to renounce the flowing movement, to turn in towards a centre, around which they then entwine themselves. Vegetable growth analogies are obvious; constantly the affinity emerges to shell and kernel, to tree rings and geological strata. With this morphology however only one side of this formal world is circumscribed: for scattered in among this rhythm of forms are countless eccentricities and extravagances — surprise motifs which check the spiral movement, divert it, stem it to form swellings or perforate it with their corrosive obstinacy. Thus arises coloured inflammation- and poisoning-processes of great fascination, in which it is not clear where a wound becomes fertilization and vice versa. These processes could be described as illustrations of an erotic alchemy. First its manifold alienations give the spiraloid rhythm its poetic dimension, at the same time they allow its absorbing power to become visual. Now we recognize the spiral as the subtle instrument of a formal will, which with richly surprising constancy — which is only ostensibly a contradiction in terms — manages literally to "embody" everything: the green rectangle of the meadow and the steamer, the tear and the raindrop, the bicycle and the prison yard, the hump-backed church and the jellyfish ship . . .

From this viewpoint the term "imagination" takes on a new field of expression: it relates less to the imagination of things and forms which do not exist in the world of experience, but rather describes, precisely among the phenomena of this world of experience, a now obsessional power of formal appropriation. Imagination consequently becomes the abiliy to assimilate a multitude of realities, both bizarre and everyday, into a kind of overlapping rhythm, i. e. to incorporate them into the picture (to "imagine" them).

Further conclusions can be drawn from this. Hundertwasser has much in common with the old Roman soothsayers, the diviners of entrails. He records past and future assimilation processes of the world body, he makes us witnesses of many-layered entrail constellations. But these are not the exalted "inner halls of the world" such as appeared to Rilke, but coloured kaleidoscope landscapes, which are built and nourished from the umbilical cord of the spiral. Here a temporal dimension emerges: the glance penetrates into slowly unfolding geological strata, in which natural forms and relics of civilsation exist side by side -— and yet the competent experts — the geologists, historians and archaeologists — would not find it easy to fit their finds into the customary categories. The wealth of allusion which Hundertwasser invests in his pictures often employs startling effects. The refined stands side by side with the primitives, which is nonetheless exquisite in its effect; delicate shades contrast with signal garishness, mild tones of weathering and decay can unexpectedly stray into poisonous colour aggressions, and many linear intricacies are reminiscent of tentacles which could just as well have originated from fauna as from flora.

The slow, careful execution of the painting process is related to the temporal dimension and at the same time indicates that the lines not only have the task of bringing out a nuclear zone, but should also bind it, often conceal it. This centre — which can of course also be placed eccentrically — is the place in which the picture-magic has its radiation centre. Not without reason are these zones often distinguished from the rest of the picture by being of gold and silver and thus ennobled, to become the impenetrable bearers of secrets, as in "The five arms of gold over the four seas" (plate 20). This should not be understood as a pseudo-sacralisation of a "Holy of Holies" but rather as one aspect of masking and concealment to which Hundertwasser's paintings owe much of their magic.

We have spoken of obsession. This, and the reference to the zone of magic, could help support the assumption that it is a matter here of the degeneration of the painting-act into the ritual. Certainly the devotion with which Hundertwasser takes possession of the canvas can be called unusual, as it does not let itself be hurried. Perhaps too something like self-forgetfulness may emanate from so much concentration, and also the adventurous joy in distilling and concentrating the coloured "essences" is unmistakeable. Yet this should not allow us to forget that the regulating, balancing part of the consciousness also plays a decisive role. It expresses itself in an ironic equanimity, which gives Narcissus self-detachment and guards him from letting himself be cheated by self-admiration or intuition. This lucidity makes Hundertwasser a romantic of a special stamp: not a proclaimer of irrational pathos, vaunting deep emotion, but a meditative explorer of regions which Novalis traced in his poetry. There everything is ramification and symbiosis, ingenious metamorphosis mingled with naive surprise; there the course of the world is contemplatively slowed down and at the same time illumined from a conscious distance: "The actual meaning of the history of mankind", wrote Novalis in Heinrich von Ofterdingen, "only develops later and more under the silent influences of memory than under the more powerful impressions of the present. The most recent events seem to be but loosely related, yet they sympathise in a truly wondrous way with those more distant; and only when one is in a position to look down over a long chain of events neither to take everything literally nor to confuse the actual order with wanton dreams, does one notice the secret links of the past with the future and learn to compile history out of hope and memory."

Werner Hofmann

Biographical notes

1928 Born on 15 December in Vienna (as Friedrich Sto-
wasser).

1929 His father dies.

1936 Attends Montisori school in Vienna. In his final report
special mention is made of his "extraordinary feeling
for colour and form".

1943 First serious crayon drawings. During this year sixty-
nine of his Jewish relatives on the maternal side are
deported eastwards and killed.

1948 "Matura". Three months at the Akademie der Bildenden Künste in Vienna, Schillerplatz (Andersen's class).
Lasting stimulus provided by exhibition of the painter
Kampmann in the Albertina in Vienna (Glass-tinkling
transparent winter trees). Influence of Egon Schiele.

1949 Chooses the name "Hundertwasser". Journey through
Tuscany. Ceramic tiles with melting colours in a
small café in Rome leave a strong impression.
Influence of Paul Klee.

1950   First stay in Paris. Leaves the Ecole des Beaux Arts after one day.

1951   In Morocco and Tunis. Comes to love Arab music, which he prefers to any other. From September 1951 member of the Art-Club, Vienna.

1952   Decorative-abstract period.

1953   The first spiral appears in the paintings. Second stay in Paris.

1953—56   Represented by Galerie Facchetti, Paris.

1954   September—October in the Santo Spirito Hospital in Rome with jaundice. Many watercolours painted during this period. Hundertwasser develops the theory on "transautomatism" and begins to number his pictures.

1956   In Summer signs on an Esthonian ship sailing under a Liberian flag. Further work on problems of the individual observer's "journey" through a painting. Publishes "La visibilité de la création transautomatique" in Cimaise, May 1956.

1957   Buys country home, "La Picaudière", in Normandy. Summer in St. Tropez. Carries his theory of "transautomatism" further to a "Grammer of Seeing". Awarded Prix du Syndicat d'Initiative, at Ist Biennale Bordeaux.

1957—60   Under contract to Galerie H. Kamer, Paris.

1958   Marriage in Gibraltar (divorced 1960). In July a reading of the "Verschimmelungsmanifest" at a congress in Seckau monastery, Austria, then in the Galerie van de Loo, Munich, and in the Galerie Parnass, Wuppertal.

1959   Sanbra Prize of the 5th Biennale in Sao Paulo. In Autumn guest lecturer at the Kunsthochschule der Freien und Hansestadt Hamburg. Resigns lectureship.

1961   In Japan. Mainichi Prize of the 6th International Art Exhibition, Tokyo.

1962   Marriage to Yuuko Ikewada in Vienna. Studio on the Giudecca, Venice. Great interest aroused by one man show in the Austrian pavilion at the Venice Biennale.

1963   Journey to Greece.

1964   Long stay in Hannover, where the artist prepares his exhibition at the Kestner Gesellschaft. Climbing tour in the Tirol. Essay for the exhibition in Stockholm, "35 Tage Schweden".

1965   January, journey to Stockholm, then journey to Vienna.

Exhibitions

1948   First exhibited picture at a students exhibition of the Akademie der Bildenden Künste in the Vienna Secession (October).

1949   First exhibited picture in Paris in the Galerie Librairie Palmes (October).

1951   First impact on general public aroused after the exhibition of paintings in "Das gute Bild für Jeden", Künstlerhaus, Vienna (December).

1952   First one man show in the Art-Club, Vienna (February). First one man show in Venice, Galleria Sandri (February).
Takes part in Secession, Vienna.
Österreichische Kunst der Gegenwart, Salzburg.

1953   Art-Club, Vienna (February).
Takes part in exhibition at Studio Paul Facchetti, Paris.

1954   First one man show in Paris, Studio Paul Facchetti,
présentation Julien Alvard (February).
Takes part in Venice Biennale.
IInd International Festival, Parma.

1955   First one man show in Milan, Galleria del Naviglio
Carlo Cardazzo (February).
Takes part in Salon des Réalités Nouvelles, Paris.
Premio Lissone, Milan, Rome, Turin.

1956   Galerie Paul Facchetti, Paris (March).

1957   Galerie H. Kamer, Paris (March).
Galerie H. Kamer, Cannes (Summer).
Galerie St. Stephan, Vienna (October).
·Takes part in Sao Paulo Biennale.

1958   Galerie H. Kamer, Paris (June).

1959   Takes part in Paris Biennale.
Sao Paulo Biennale.

1960   Galerie Delta, Basle (May).
Galerie Raymond Cordier, Paris (October).

1961   Tokyo Gallery, Tokyo (May).
6th International Art Exhibition, Tokyo.

1962   One man exhibition at the Venice Biennale (Summer).
Galleria La Medusa, Rome (November).
Takes part in the opening exhibition of the Museum
des 20. Jahrhunderts, Vienna (September).

1963   Galerie Anne Abels, Cologne.
Takes part in the exhibition "Idole und Dämonen" in
the Museum des 20. Jahrhunderts, Vienna (Summer).

1964   Kestner-Gesellschaft, Hannover.
Kunsthalle, Bern.
Karl-Ernst-Osthaus-Museum, Hagen.
Stedelijk-Museum, Amsterdam.

1965   Moderna Museet, Stockholm.
Museum des 20. Jahrhunderts, Vienna.
Paintings by Hundertwasser have appeared in nearly
all the international exhibitions of Austrian art since
1945, as well as at many exhibitions of the Ecole de
Paris.

List of Plates

34   THE BLIND AND CRYING CAR, 1963

35   THE NEIGHBOURS (II) —
      SPIRAL SUN AND MOONHOUSE, 1963

36   BLOOD-GARDEN —
      HOUSES WITH YELLOW SMOKE, 1962—1963

37   GREEN TOWERS IN THE SUN, 1963—1964

38   THE END OF GREECE, 1963—1964

39   THREE HOT WATER BOTTLE WINDOW TREES
      (formerly: YELLOW CITY TREES), 1963—1964
      THE DREAMS OF DORIS, 1952—1964
      SICK WINDOW, 1959—1964
      (working condition)

40   THE BURNING BALD-HEAD

41   GREEN SPIRAL AT HOME, 1964

42   THE HAIRDRESSER'S HEAVEN, 1964

43   RUN IN THE SUN, 1964

Plates

1 MANY TRANSPARENT HEADS, 1949—1950
   Watercolour, 1949/1950, 37x25 cm
   W-Kat. No 570, upright format
   Owner: Dr. Alfred Schmeller, Vienna.

2 **PART OF A STEAMER (1)**

Watercolour, St. Mandé/Seine 1950, 52x74 cm
W-Kat. No. 87, oblong format
Owner: Mrs. J. S. McLean, Toronto

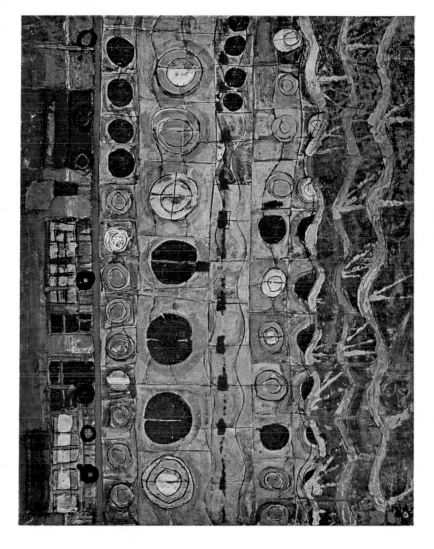

3 **IN MEZZO AL MARE (ON THE HIGH SEAS)**
   SINGING STEAMER (II)

Watercolour, Rettenegg 1950, 59x68 cm
W-Kat. No. 101, oblong format

Owner: Siegfried Poppe, Hamburg.

The inspiration for this picture was an Italian waifs'
song.

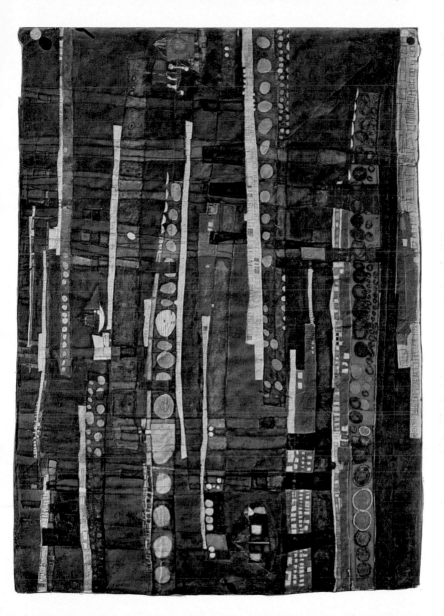

4 DEVOURING FISHES AND CYCLISTS
Watercolour, Marrakesh 1951, finished in Vienna,
Tragöss and Anguillara 1962, 47x60 cm
W-Kat. No. 114, oblong format
Owner: Dr. Weinbrenner, Opladen

5 PORTRAIT OF ROSLYN (III)

Watercolour, Marrakesh 1951, 30x25 cm
W-Kat. No. 113, upright format
Owner: Roslyn Robles, Paris

6 **FRONT VIEW OF STEAMER**

Watercolour, Hofgastein 1951, 30x50 cm
W-Kat. No. 123, oblong format
Owner: Dr. Wilhelm Mack, Vienna

7 **SUMMERHOUSE FRAME WITH HEADS AND A CAR**
Watercolour, Vienna 1952, 38x66 cm
W-Kat. No. 141, oblong format
Owner: Max Lersch, Vienna

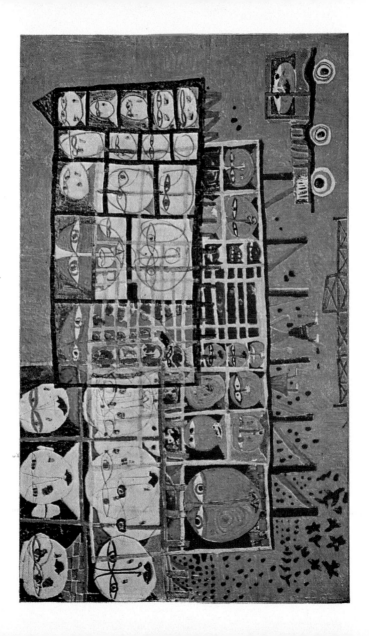

8   THE INVASIONS

Watercolour, Vienna 1952, 78x89 cm
W-Kat. No. 152, oblong format

Owner: Dr. Otto Domnick, Stuttgart

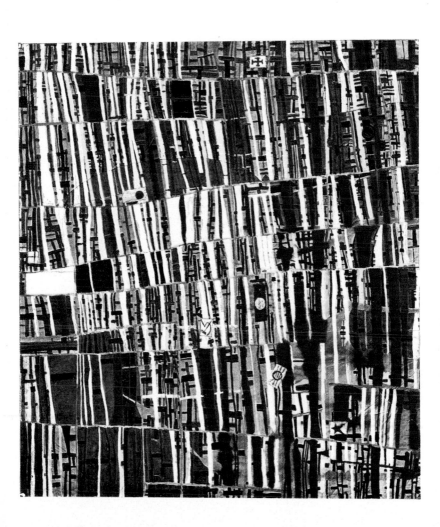

9 **HOUSE OF ARCADES AND YELLOW TOWER**
   Watercolour, Saint Maurice/Seine 1953, 124x90 cm
   W-Kat. No. 165, upright format
   Owner: Shinichi Tajiri, Holland-USA

10 THE GARDEN OF THE HAPPY DEAD

Oil on hardboard, Saint Maurice/Seine 1953, 47x58,5 cm
W-Kat. No. 170, oblong format

Owner: Inna Salomon, Paris

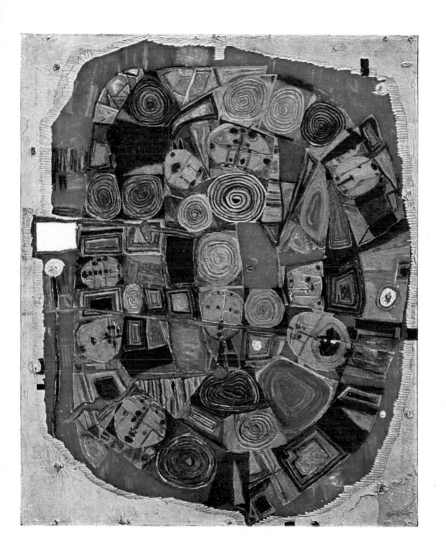

11 ARAB GEOGRAPHER WITH SATELLITE
Oil on hardboard, Saint Maurice/Seine 1953, 58x55 cm
with square added at bottom left 13x12,5 cm
W-Kat. No. 174, upright format
Owner: Mariuccia Toninelli, Milan

12 A CORNER OF GERMAN EARTH

Watercolour, Rome, Ospedale di Santo Spirito 1954,
35x53 cm

W-Kat. No. 190, oblong format

Owner: Galerie Änne Abels, Cologne

13 HEAD WITH WHITE WINDOWS

Watercolour, Rome, Ospedale di Santo Spirito 1954,
18x27 cm
W-Kat. No. 193, oblong format
Owner: Dr. Alfred Schmeller, Vienna

14 **MAGIC CUBE**

Watercolour, Vienna, Universitätsklinik 1954, 28x34 cm
W-Kat. No. 209, oblong format

Owner: Dr. Wilhelm Mack, Vienna

15 THE ISLAND

Synthetic Resin, Vienna 1955, 58x72 cm
W-Kat. No. 208, oblong format

Owner: Österreichische Galerie im Oberen Belvedere,
Vienna

16 SINGING STEAMER (III)

Watercolour, St. Jakob in Tirol 1956, 46x55 cm
W-Kat. No. 263, oblong format

Owner: formely Willi Verkauf, Vienna

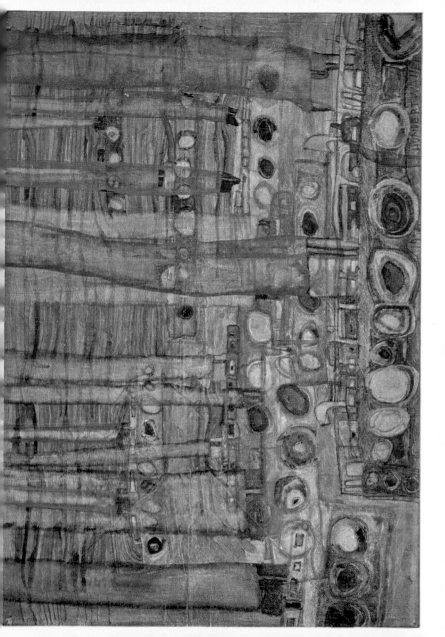

17 GARDEN WITH HALO

Mixed technique, Paris 1956, 35x44 cm
W-Kat. No. 280, oblong format

Owner: James Wise, Tourrettes-sur-Loup

18 THE WAVES OF THE HEDGEHOG

Watercolour, Vienna 1957, 47,5x62 cm
W-Kat. No. 290, oblong format

Owner: Print-room of the Akademie der bildenden
Künste, Vienna

19 **LEAN PICTURE ON THE FAT OF THE GENERAL BY HANS NEUFFER (Overpainting of old picture)**

W-Kat. No. 307, upright format
Mixed technique, Saint Mandé/Seine 1957, 81x65 cm

Owner: Alexander Hollaender, Oak Ridge

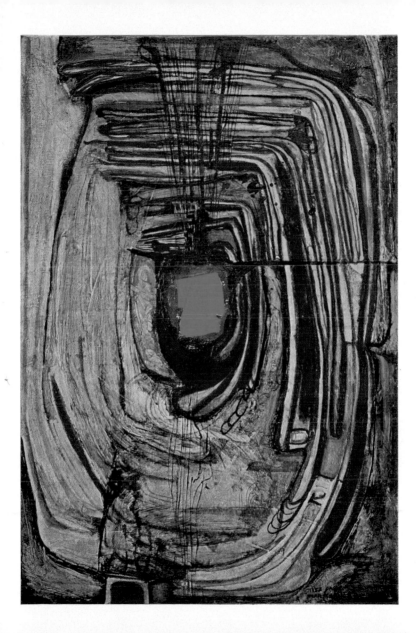

20 THE FIVE ARMS OF GOLD OVER THE FOUR SEAS

Mixed technique, Cannes, Chateau Scott 1957,
completed Paris 1959, 48x63 cm
W-Kat. No. 324, oblong format
Owner: P. T. Nielsen, Holte

21 THE YELLOW RIVER —
THE BEAUTIFUL TONGUE-TIP

Mixed technique, Paris-Vienna 1957, overpainted
Paris 1960, restored and completed La Picaudière 1963,
48x63 cm
W-Kat. No. 325, oblong format
Owner: Mme. Marteau, Paris

22 **EYE SCALES (IV)**

   Mixed technique, Sichtigvor (Möhne) 1958, 54x65 cm
   W-Kat. No. 368, oblong format

   Owner: Mme. Naude, Paris

23   CAR WITH RED RAINDROPS (IV)

Watercolour, Stockholm-Copenhagen-La Picaudière
1958, 30x65 cm
W-Kat. No. 374, oblong format
Owner: Architect Fred Freyler, Vienna

**24 SATISFIED SUN —
THE MELTING HALF-MOUNTAIN**

Mixed technique, La Picaudière 1959, 60x73 cm
W-Kat. No. 451, oblong format

Owner: Galerie Moos, Geneva

The artist gave the second title to the picture
turned upside down

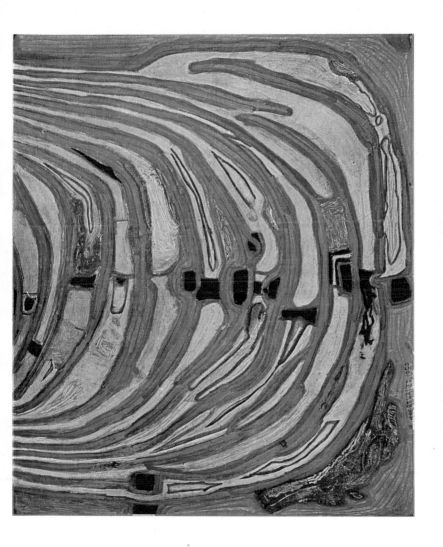

25 **THE RAIN**

Mixed technique, La Picaudière 1959, 80x60 cm
W-Kat. No. 453, upright format
Owner: Galerie Krugier, Geneva

26 **ANIMAL ON FEET**

Mixed technique, Vienna-Hamburg 1958/1959, 65x81 cm
W-Kat. No. 423, oblong format
Owner: Galerie Krugier, Geneva

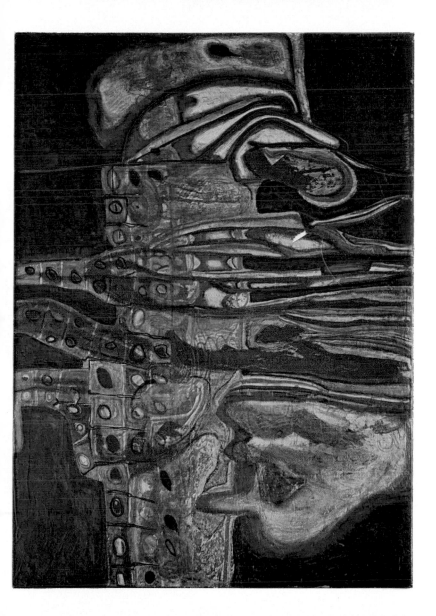

27 **COCKSCOMB**

Watercolour, Kolding-Denmark-Hamburg 1959,
W-Kat. No. 428, upright format
64x50 cm

Owner: Claude Fievet, Paris

28 MAN CRYING IN SPIRALS
Watercolour, Vienna 1960, 65x48 cm
W-Kat. No. 427, upright format
Owner: Richard Dreyfus, Basle

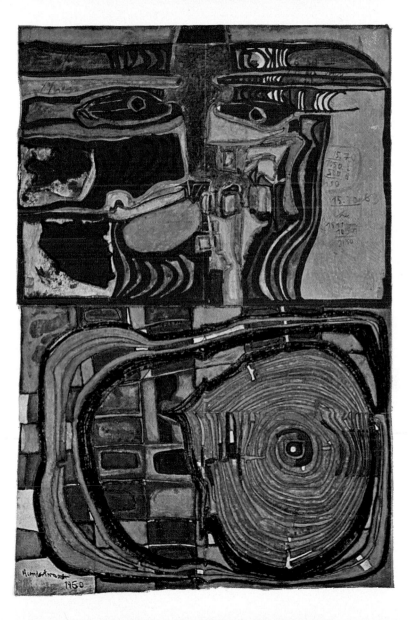

29   THE I DON'T KNOW YET

Mixed technique, La Picaudière 1960, 130x195 cm
W-Kat. No. 433, oblong format

Owner: Jacqueline Descamps, Brussels

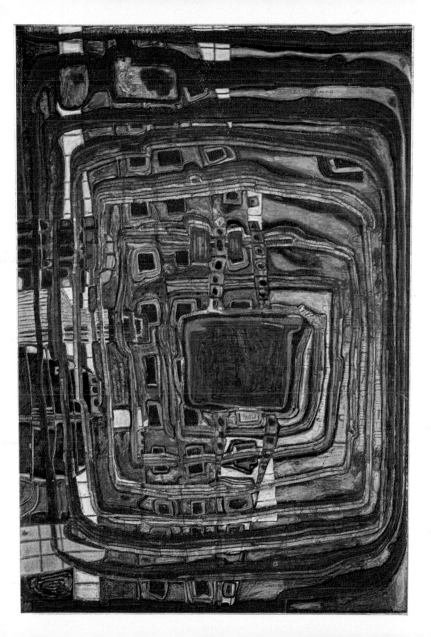

30   BLACK, BURIED EYE

W-Kat. No. 426, oblong format
Mixed technique, Paris 1960, 54x65 cm
Owner: Marquis de Segur, Paris

31 HOUSES IN THE SNOW IN SILVER RAIN

Watercolour, snowed in a guesthouse in Piano del
Voglio in the Apennines 1962, 68x51 cm
W-Kat. No. 557, upright format

Owner: Julian J. and Joachim Jean Aberbach,
New York

32 **THE BEARD IS THE GRASS OF THE BALD**
    Mixed technique, La Picaudière 1961, 114x146 cm
    W-Kat. No. 498, oblong format
    Property of the artist

33   THE FEET OF KAORU

**Watercolour, beach-hut in Zushi-Higashi Nagasaki,
Hyakusen Ryokan, Tokyo 1961, 26x48 cm
W-Kat. No. 486, oblong format**

Owner: Tokyo Gallery, Tokyo

**TWO NAIL MOUNTAINS BY THE GREEN POND —
THE DREAM OF NANCY**

**Watercolour, Nancy-Paris 1962, 29x33 cm
W-Kat. No. 520, oblong format**

Owner: Carl Flinker, Paris

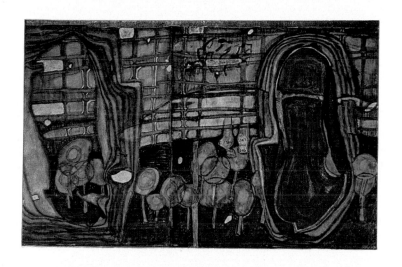

34 THE BLIND AND CRYING CAR

Mixed technique, La Picaudière 1963, 65x81 cm
W-Kat. No. 550, oblong format

Owner: Siegfried Adler, Montagnola

35 **THE NEIGHBOURS (II) —**
    SPIRAL SUN AND MOONHOUSE

Mixed technique, La Picaudière 1963, 65x81 cm
W-Kat. No. 552, oblong format

Owner: Karl-Ernst and Hildegard Oertel, Düsseldorf

36 BLOOD-GARDEN —
HOUSES WITH YELLOW SMOKE

Mixed technique, Vienna-Venice 1962/1963, 81x65 cm
W-Kat. No. 564, upright format

Owner: Julian J. and Joachim Jean Aberbach,
New York

37 **GREEN TOWERS IN THE SUN**
   Mixed technique, border station Eidomeni-Orient
   Express Belgrad-Vrsar-Triest-Venice, September 1963;
   Giudecca, October 1963; Zorge im Harz, February 1964,
   51x73 cm
   W-Kat. No. 584, oblong format
   Owner: Dieter and Edith Rosenkranz, Wuppertal

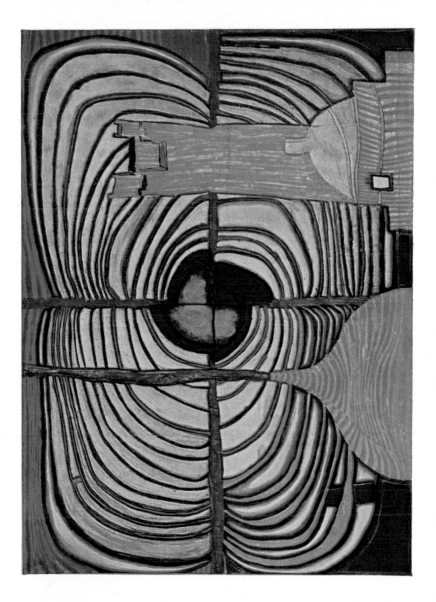

38 **THE END OF GREECE**

Mixed technique, Delphi-Herakleon on S/S
Delos-Santorini-Mykonos, September 1963; Giudecca,
October 1963; Hannover, February 1964, 67x48 cm
W-Kat. No. 585, upright format

Owner: Hella Grobe, Isernhagen

**39 THREE HOT WATER BOTTLE WINDOW TREES
(formerly: YELLOW CITY TREES)**

Mixed technique, Venice 1963 - Hannover 1964,
14x24 cm

W-Kat. No. 588, oblong format

Owner: Dr. Wieland Schmied, Hannover

THE DREAMS OF DORIS

Mixed technique, Vienna 1952, Paris 1959, Venice 1963,
Hannover 1964, two former pieces from "La Lune en
Rodage", 24x13 cm

W-Kat. No. 589, upright format

Owner: Dr. Hans Rohkrämer, Mühlheim/Ruhr

**SICK WINDOW
(working condition)**

Mixed technique, Paris 1959, Giudecca 1963, Hannover
1964, 15,5x22,5 cm

W-Kat. No. 587, oblong format

Property of the artist

40 THE BURNING BALD-HEAD

Mixed technique, Vienna-Radschin, Waldviertel, 1962,
73 × 92 cm
W-Kat. No. 516, oblong format
Owner: Siegfried Poppe, Hamburg

41 GREEN SPIRAL AT HOME

Mixed technique, altered during various journeys in
Europe, completed Venice 1964, 78x50 cm
W-Kat. No. 591, upright format

Owner: Emilio Arditti, Paris

A copy of Lithograph No. 305, overpainted with
watercolour in 1958 and completed in several stages
with egg tempera.

42 **THE HAIDRESSER'S HEAVEN**

Watercolour, Hannover-Hamburg-La Picaudière 1964,
broadest measurements 43,5x41,5 cm
W-Kat. No. 601, upright format
Owner: Karl Ströher, Darmstadt

43 **RUN IN THE SUN**

Watercolour, Hamburg-Neustadt-Steinhude-Hannover
1964, Neu Harlingersiel, Venice, Kassel 1964, 36x100 cm
W-Kat. No. 602, oblong format

Owner: P. T. Nielsen, Holte

44 SUNSET

Watercolour, Brussels-Munich-Salzburg 1964, 26x33 cm
W-Kat. No. 603, oblong format

Owner: Juuko Ikewada, Venice

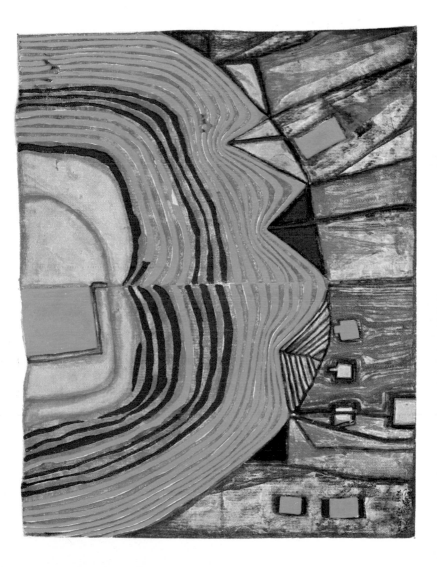

45 LANDSCAPE BY THE SILVER RIVER

Mixed technique, painted while on a climbing tour in the
Tirol, completed Venice 1964, 50x57 cm

W-Kat. No. 605, oblong format

Owner: Änne Abels, Cologne

**46   KONRAD BAYER'S DEATH —
HANA NO HANA —
THE NOSE FLOWER**

Mixed technique, Zillertal Alps-Schloß Hagenberg-
Giudecca 1964, 57x50 cm

W-Kat. No. 606, upright format

Property of the artist

This picture is a curious premonition of Konrad Bayer's
suicide

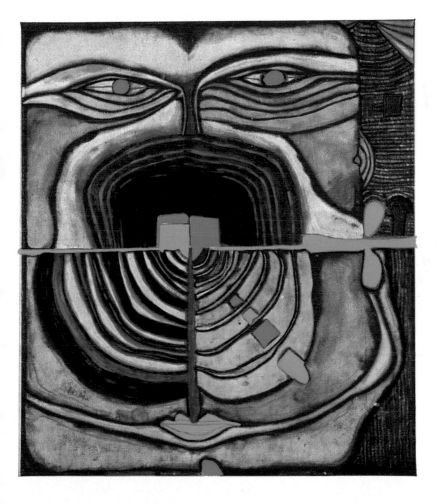

47 SHIPWRECK —
THE DECLINE OF VENICE

Mixed technique, started on a voyage from Venice to
Rhodes, September 1964, completed Giudecca, October
1964, 68,5x49 cm
W-Kat. No. 609, upright format
Owner: Dr. Bernhard Sprengel, Hannover

**48 THE END OF THE GREEKS —
THE OSTROGOTHS AND THE VISIGOTHS**

Mixed technique, started on a voyage from Rhodes to
Venice, September 1964, completed Venice, October 1964,
49x68,5 cm

W-Kat. No. 608, oblong format

Owner: Siegfried and Gesche Poppe, Hamburg

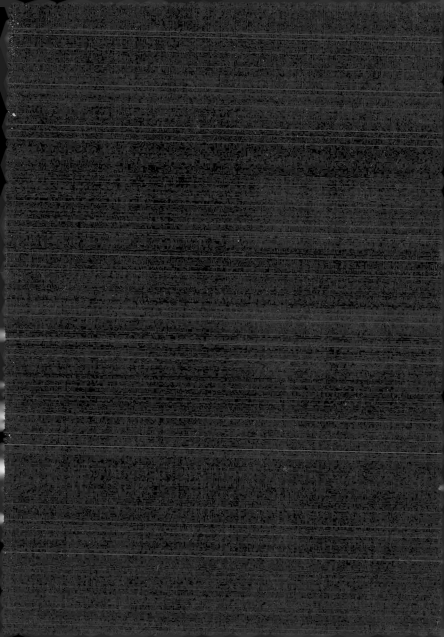